Real Radio

A Play

Jonny Zucker

Illustrated by
Paul Savage

Titles in Full Flight Variety

Abducted by an Alien	Jonny Zucker
Summer Trouble	Jonny Zucker
Sleepwalker	Jillian Powell
The Reactor	Jillian Powell
Starship Football	David Orme
Race of a Lifetime	Tony Norman
Speedway	Tony Norman
Goalkeepers	Jonny Zucker
Your Passing Was Rubbish and other poems	ed. Jonny Zucker
Real Radio – A Play	Jonny Zucker

Badger Publishing Limited
Oldmedow Road, Hardwick Industrial Estate,
King's Lynn PE30 4JJ
Telephone: 01438 791037
www.badgerlearning.co.uk

2 4 6 8 10 9 7 5 3

Real Radio – A Play   ISBN 978 1 85880 930 4
First edition © 2002
This second edition © 2013

Text © Jonny Zucker 2002
Series editing © Jonny Zucker 2002
Complete work © Badger Publishing Limited 2002

All rights reserved. No part of this publication may be reproduced, stored in any form or by any means mechanical, electronic, recording or otherwise without the prior permission of the publisher.

The right of Jonny Zucker to be identified as author of this Work has been asserted by him in accordance with the Copyright, Designs and Patents Act 1988.

Series Editor: Jonny Zucker.
Publisher: David Jamieson.
Editor: Paul Martin.
Cover design: Jain Birchenough.
Cover illustration: Paul Savage.

Real Radio

A Play

Jonny Zucker

Illustrated by Paul Savage

Contents

Characters		4
Scene 1	The Playground	5
Scene 2	The Maths Room, After School	10
Scene 3	By the Gates After School	17
Scene 4	Outside the School Canteen, the Next Day at Morning Break	22
Scene 5	The Maths Room, that Afternoon	27

Characters

Miss Potts – OK teacher

Mr Denton – Head Teacher

Spud – Techno Wizard

James – All mouth

Kate – Girl DJ

Dean – Moaner

Scene 1 – The Playground

Spud, James, Kate and Dean are sitting on their favourite bench.

James: Real Radio is going to be the best radio station in the country.

Dean: Don't be silly. It's only a school radio station.

James: Yeah, but we've got the top team. It's going to be the best.

Dean: I think you're getting a bit excited.

Kate: Can you two stop fighting? There's so much to do.

Spud: Kate's right. We've got to get all of the gear up those stairs and into the maths room.

James: Let's do it after school today. I bet Miss Potts will give us a hand.

Dean: No she won't. She's always busy.

Spud: After school sounds good to me, let's ask Miss Potts at lunchtime.

Miss Potts wanders over to the bench.

Miss Potts: Ask Miss Potts what?

Kate: Oh, hi Miss. We were just wondering if it would be okay to move all of the stuff for Real Radio up into the maths room after school.

Miss Potts: Yes okay, I'll help you, but there may be a small problem.

Spud: What sort of problem?

Miss Potts: The Head Teacher, Mr Denton, isn't too sure about Real Radio. He wants to keep a very close eye on all of you.

Dean: Told you it wouldn't work.

Miss Potts: No I think it will work, but you need to show him how serious you are about it.

Kate: But we are serious, Miss. My CDs are my whole life.

Miss Potts: I know, Kate, you don't have to prove anything to me. I'm just telling you how it is.

James: Okay Miss, we get the message, now how about after school?

Miss Potts: After school's fine, meet me outside the staff room.

Miss Potts walks off.

Dean: Mr Denton's going to give us all sorts of hassle.

James: Rubbish! By the time we show him what we can do, he'll love it.

The bell rings.

Scene 2 –
The Maths Room, After School

Spud, James, Dean, Kate and Miss Potts are putting lots of bags on the floor.

Dean: That stuff was so heavy. My back really hurts.

James: But we've done it! All the stuff is here and we're ready to set up.

Kate: I want to know where all of my CDs are. I can't find the case.

Spud: Yeah. Where's my bag with all of those wires in? I can't see it anywhere.

Miss Potts: Will you all calm down! All of your stuff is here. We just carried it up the stairs. What we need to do is sort everything out, and put it on those tables over there.

They start taking things out of the bags and putting them on the tables.

Kate: Brilliant! I've found my CDs. I can't wait until Real Radio is up and running.

Dean: If we *get* it up and running. There's so much stuff here. It just looks like a mess.

Spud: Don't worry Dean. We'll sort it out.

Miss Potts: That's right. We can put Kate's CDs over here, and all of Spud's bits and pieces over there.

James: I can just see it. We'll win the school radio station of the year prize. They'll want to talk to us for the local newspaper.

Kate: Yeah, yeah James, dream on.

Spud: Hey Dean, can you just press that blue switch over there?

Dean presses the green switch by mistake. There's a puff of smoke and then a cranking sound. All of the power in the room goes off.

Spud: YOU IDIOT! YOU'VE JUST FUSED THE POWER!

Dean: YOU'RE THE IDIOT. YOU TOLD ME TO PRESS THE SWITCH!

Spud: BUT YOU PRESSED THE WRONG SWITCH!

Spud runs across the room, flicks a few buttons and the power comes back on again.

Spud: IDIOT!

Dean: FOOL!

Miss Potts: WILL YOU TWO STOP SHOUTING AT EACH OTHER!

The door is flung open and Mr Denton walks in looking very cross.

Mr Denton (*angrily*): So this is why my computer suddenly turned off.

When it switched itself back on, I found out that I'd just lost the whole of my Head Teacher's report.

Miss Potts: I'm so sorry Mr Denton, it was just a little mistake.

Spud (*whispering*): You should have saved it.

Mr Denton: What did you say?

Spud: Nothing Mr Denton.

Mr Denton: Well I'm very sorry everyone, but after this 'little mistake,' I don't feel I can trust any of you…

From now on, Real Radio is off!

Mr Denton walks out, leaving everyone in the room looking very shocked.

Scene 3 – By the Gates After School

Dean: I told you it would never work. It's your fault.

Spud: You must be joking. You shouldn't have pressed the wrong switch.

Kate: Will you two be quiet for one minute? You're driving me mad. No one is to blame. It was a mistake.

James: I agree with Kate. If we're going to make this the best radio station in the country, we have to work together.

Dean: There won't be any radio station. Didn't you hear what Mr Denton said? He looked so angry.

Kate: I haven't ever seen him looking that cross. Even Miss Potts was shocked.

James: Talking of Miss Potts, there she is about to get into her car.

Dean, Spud, James and Kate run over to her car.

Miss Potts: Oh, it's you lot. That didn't work out very well did it?

Spud: Sorry Miss, we've blown it haven't we?

Miss Potts: You can say that again!

James: I still think it can work out. Someone needs to have a brilliant idea. Something that will change Mr Denton's mind.

Dean: Forget about it. There's no chance he'll ever change his mind.

Kate: Hang on a second. I've just had a great idea, but I need to speak to Miss Potts in private.

Spud: What are you on about?

Kate: Just give us a minute, okay?

Dean, Spud and James walk away from the car. Kate whispers something to Miss Potts. Miss Potts scratches her head and after a few seconds starts laughing. She then gets into her car and drives away.

James: What do you think Kate said to her?

Spud: Haven't got a clue.

Dean: Nor have I.

Kate walks back over to join them.

Spud: What was all that about then?

Kate: Never you mind. You'll find out in good time.

They all start walking home together.

Scene 4 –
Outside the School Canteen, the Next Day at Morning Break

Spud and James are sitting on a wall, Kate and Dean are standing.

Dean: We'll have to find something else to do.

James: I still think we can make a go of Real Radio.

Spud: I think this time Dean may be right. Mr Denton was so angry with us in the maths room yesterday. I think we might as well forget about it.

James: What do you think Kate?

Kate: I'm waiting.

Dean: What are you waiting for?

Miss Potts walks over to them.

Miss Potts: I think she might be waiting for me. Is that right Kate?

Kate: Yes, Miss. Is there any news?

Miss Potts: Yes Kate, I do have some news.

Dean: I bet it's more bad news. I bet Mr Denton wants to see us at lunchtime or call our parents in because of yesterday.

Miss Potts: It's good news in fact, Dean.

Spud, Dean and James: Good news?

Miss Potts: It seems that Mr Denton has changed his mind about Real Radio.

Spud: Are you joking Miss? He lost the report on his computer. He was so angry.

Miss Potts: I'm not joking, Spud. He says you can set the whole thing up at lunchtime and do your first show this afternoon.

James: This can't be true!

Miss Potts: It is true, James. He's even said that every class can have a speaker in their classroom, and that all lessons can stop for twenty minutes so the whole school can hear your show.

Spud: You must have magic powers, Miss. Thanks a lot!

Miss Potts: You don't need to thank me. It's all down to Kate.

Spud, James and Dean turn to look at Kate.

Spud: What's this all about Kate? What did you whisper to Miss Potts by her car yesterday?

Kate: Forget about that now. Let's get back to class. As soon as this lesson is over we can get on with setting up Real Radio!

Kate, Spud, James and Dean start to run back to their class.

Miss Potts: Don't run in the corridor!

Scene 5 – The Maths Room, that Afternoon

Spud is pushing some buttons on a long, black machine with lots of lights. Dean is walking around the room. Miss Potts is standing in the corner of the room. Kate and James are sitting at a table in front of a microphone. There is another microphone on the other side of the table, and an empty chair opposite them.

James: I still don't know how you and Miss Potts were able to pull this off.

Dean: Don't get too excited. Something might still go wrong.

Miss Potts: There's no chance of that Dean. Everything is taken care of.

Spud (*flicking a last button*): Okay everyone. We're ready to go. Is everyone okay?

Spud, James, Kate and Dean all nod.

Spud: Alright then. Kate you're on first. Five, four, three, two, one, let's do it.

Kate: Hi, and good afternoon everyone and welcome to Real Radio – our school's very own radio station.

James: It's great to have you all listening in your classrooms.

Kate: And we're going to begin our first ever show with a very special guest.

Spud (*whispering*): Guest? What's she talking about?

The door opens and Mr Denton walks in.

Spud, James and Dean all look very surprised.

Dean (*whispering*): Oh no! He's changed his mind and he's going to stop us!

Kate: Good afternoon Mr Denton.

Mr. Denton (*sitting down in the empty chair*): Good afternoon, Kate. And may I say first of all, how superb you've all made this room look. It looks like a proper radio station.

Spud (*whispering*): It is a proper radio station.

James: We'd all like to say thanks for letting us run Real Radio, Mr Denton. We thought it might not ever happen.

Mr Denton: Well at first I wasn't sure about the idea of a station, and I nearly stopped the whole thing happening. But then Miss Potts told me that Kate had suggested I should be the very first guest on your show. I could hardly say no to that!

Dean, Spud and James all suddenly smile at Kate.

Dean (*whispering*): Brilliant idea.

Kate winks back at them and gives a thumbs-up to Miss Potts.

Kate: Now, it's time for the first song…

And just before I play it
Mr Denton, have you got a
message for everyone who is
listening?

Mr Denton: Yes I have. My message to
everyone is – always save
your work on the computer!

Kate (*smiling*): OK Mr Denton! Well,
I've chosen a song that I
know loads of you out there
really like. And don't forget:
listening to Real Radio is far
better than doing any work!

Kate presses 'play'. The first beats of a song are heard all round the school.

THE END